W9-CGL-514

SEARCHING FOR DAVID'S HEART

A Play in Two Acts

by

CHERIE BENNETT

Adapted from *Searching for David's Heart*,
also by Cherie Bennett (Scholastic Books, 1998)

* winner, 1999 Aurand Harris Memorial Children's Playwriting
  Award
* winner, 1998 New Visions/New Voices biennial, The Kennedy
  Center
* winner, 2000 American Alliance of Theater and Education
  Unpublished Play Reading Project
* certificate of award, 1999 Bonderman biennial

Dramatic Publishing
Woodstock, Illinois • England • Australia • New Zealand

*** **NOTICE** ***

Under the auspices of the Long Wharf Theatre (New Haven, Connecticut) this play was a winner of The Kennedy Center's biennial New Visions/New Voices 1998 project, a forum for works-in-progress, and presented at The Kennedy Center in May 1998.

For Jeff, my partner in art as well as in life; my biggest booster and toughest critic, and dramaturge, who so often sees what I miss and brings me to the truth...sometimes more easily than other times!

Grateful acknowledgment to the following people and institutions: Scholastic, Inc, New York; The Long Wharf Theatre, New Haven, Connecticut; Appleton Wisconsin Historical Society and Houdini Museum; Appleton Wisconsin Public Library; Wisconsin State Patrol, Madison, Wisconsin; Fr. Fernand J. Cheri III, St. Vincent de Paul Church, Nashville, Tennessee; Rev. Forrest Harris, Pleasant Green Missionary Baptist Church, Nashville; Rabbi Stephen Fuchs, Congregation Beth Israel, West Hartford, Connecticut; Angela Cowser, Tying Nashville Together, Nashville; Vanderbilt University Children's Hospital Transplant Unit, Nashville; United Network for Organ Sharing, Richmond, Virginia.

IMPORTANT BILLING AND CREDIT REQUIREMENTS

All producers of the play *must* give credit to the author(s) of the play in all programs distributed in connection with performances of the play and in all instances in which the title of the play appears for purposes of advertising, publicizing or otherwise exploiting the play and/or a production. The name of the author(s) *must* also appear on a separate line, on which no other name appears, immediately following the title, and *must* appear in size of type not less than fifty percent the size of the title type. Biographical information on the author(s), if included in this book, may be used on all programs. *On all programs this notice must appear:*

"Produced by special arrangement with
THE DRAMATIC PUBLISHING COMPANY of Woodstock, Illinois"

SEARCHING FOR DAVID'S HEART

A Play in Two Acts

For 10 actors (4f, 6m, with doubling as indicated below.)
The play can be done with a cast of 9 (3f, 6m) by eliminating the role of Linda (line changes available from the playwright), and having only Winston's father present.

CHARACTERS

FEMALE ROLES

DARCY (DEE DEE) DEETON: Age 12. Small for her age.

CLAIRE DEETON: Darcy's mom. A nurse.
   Doubles as ENID MANNERS: Older, gullible.
   Passenger on the bus.

DR. LINDA PAWLING: Winston's mom. A pediatrician.
   Can double as DR. LEE.

CRYSTAL EVANS: Age 17, David's girlfriend, lovely.
   Can double as AMANDA BLISS: Age 13, a classmate;
   also as CHARLENE: Age 18, an escape artist's assistant.

MALE ROLES

SAM WEISS: Age 12, Darcy's best friend and soulmate.
   Even smaller than Darcy.

HARRY HOUDINI: The one and only consummate showman.
   He also plays many other roles as indicated. He is not
   doubling and is always obviously recognizable as Houdini.

DOUG DEETON: Darcy's dad. A cop.

AARON WEISS: Sam's dad. A public defender lawyer. Can double as DR. JOHN PAUL PAWLING: Winston's dad. A doctor.

DAVID DEETON: Age 18. Darcy's brother. Can double as AMAZIN' EDDIE: Age 18. Second-rate escape artist.

WINSTON PAWLING: Age 12, but could look younger.

Everyone but Darcy, Sam, Enid, Amazin' Eddie and Charlene can double as audience in carnival scenes. The non-speaking, motionless role of Meemaw can be played by any actor of the director's choice. We never see her face.

TIME: The present.

PLACE: Appleton, Wisconsin; on the road; Miami, Florida; a Wisconsin airport.

NOTES FROM THE PLAYWRIGHT

HOUDINI: The one and only Harry Houdini is our narrator and facilitator. As Houdini, the audience sees him, the characters do not. He alone breaks the fourth wall and weaves in and out of scenes at the discretion of the director, even joining the action at some points to play various small roles. No effort should be made to hide the fact that it is Houdini playing another role, e.g., a lady selling raffle tickets. He is allowing us, the audience, in on his great performance. A pegboard with various simple costume elements might be available for his use. While bigger than life, Houdini must never be allowed to become the focal point of the play.

DOUBLING: Except for Houdini, doubling should be disguised.

STYLE/SETS: The play flows seamlessly from one scene to the next unless otherwise indicated. Because of this flow and the varied locations, sets can be minimal. Upstage could be a large platform with usable space underneath. This platform is used as a Ferris wheel, tree house, etc.

RUNNING TIME: The act break noted is for convenience only; this play can be performed without an intermission.

MUSIC: All music is suggested only.

ACT ONE

SETTING: *Upstage: a large multipurpose platform. Stage right: a coat rack from which hang various simple costume elements—hats, wigs, etc. A trunk, some boxes, and large screen are used in various ways for all sets. The play flows from scene to scene seamlessly except where indicated.*

AT RISE: *A Sunday afternoon, September. DARCY (DEE DEE) DEETON and SAM WEISS, best friends, are holding a seance in a room lit by a red-flame candle. SAM tries to summon the spirit of the Great Houdini.*

SAM *(eyes closed, dramatically)*. O Great Houdini—
DARCY *(eyes closed, highly dubious)*. O Great Houdini—
SAM. O Powerful Houdini—
DARCY *(very "let's get it over with")*. O Powerful Houdini—
SAM. O Great One, the most incredible, unbelievable magician and escape artist that ever lived in the history of history—
DARCY *(opens eyes)*. Sucking up to the dead is pointless, Sam, OK?
SAM. K-O. *(A beat, as he shifts tactics)*. O Great Houdini, I, the Great Samdini, can now do your most famous es-

9

cape trick, Metamorphosis, better than you ever did it, and—

DARCY. Wrong. That's never gonna get him to show up.

SAM *(opens eyes, matter of fact).* Anger might jar him from The Great Beyond, you never know. His ego was out of control. *(Back into seance mode.)* O Former Greatest Escape Artist who ever lived, if your spirit is here, give us a sign by making the candle flicker now. *(They wait. Nothing happens.)*

DARCY. Maybe he doesn't like you telling him what to do.

SAM. If your spirit is here, give us a sign of your choice. *(They wait again. Nothing.)* If your spirit is here—

DARCY. It isn't.

SAM. It might be.

DARCY. It isn't. *(She blows out the candle and flips on a light.)* You can't talk to the dead, Sam. No one can. We've got homework.

SAM *(booming Samdini voice).* The Great Samdini does not do homework. *(Normal voice.)* Let's work on the Metamorphosis trick.

DARCY. Homework first, Metamorphosis trick second.

SAM. Metamorphosis first, homework second.

(He opens the trunk, takes out handcuffs and ropes, handcuffs himself, and kneels in the trunk, as DARCY takes a sheet of paper from her pocket.)

DARCY. Homework first. I need to work on my speech.

SAM. Deed, you need to get in the trunk.

DARCY. I hate the trunk.

SAM. Metamorphosis depends on it. Let's review. Handcuffed, I get in the trunk. You rope and lock the trunk. In mere seconds, I miraculously exit the trunk while you, my lowly assistant—

DARCY. Watch it!

SAM. —my lovely, lowly assistant, get inside, without disturbing the ropes or the lock. How do they do it, folks? Metamorphosis. Noun. A—

DARCY. —Change of form or character. You told me.

SAM *(lowers the trunk lid on himself)*. See? Nothing to it.

DARCY. I'm not doing it, OK?

(SAM pops up, uncuffs himself and steps out of the trunk, closing it behind him.)

SAM. K-O. And please, don't blame yourself just because you've ruined my career and my entire life.

DARCY. I won't. I hate Ms. Clark's guts. Why do I have to give a speech in front of the whole class? I'd rather eat snot.

SAM. Ms. Clark is malevolent. Adjective. Wishing harm to others. Your speech?

(He motions DARCY to stand on the trunk and give her speech. She reluctantly climbs up, hesitates, then climbs down.)

DARCY. You first.

SAM *(from memory, very been-there-done-that)*. The Person I Admire Most, by Sam Weiss. The person I admire most is the Great Harry Houdini. He grew up right here in Appleton, Wisconsin, we're both Jewish, and his last name was also Weiss before he changed it to Houdini.

(During SAM's speech, the GREAT HOUDINI rises, bound, from inside the trunk. He easily frees himself and climbs jauntily out. He sees and hears all, but can't be seen or heard by DARCY and SAM.)

SAM. Coincidence? I think not. He was formerly the greatest escape artist who ever lived. That is, until me, the
  Great Samdini.

HOUDINI. And you talk about my ego, kid!

SAM. I'm mastering all his tricks, so when I'm rich and
  famous and all you mere mortals who ever made fun of
  me are begging for my autograph, for which I will make
  you grovel, I will owe it all to my mentor, the Great
  Houdini. Thank you.

HOUDINI *(wryly)*. You're welcome.

SAM. Now do yours.

DARCY *(anything to avoid the speech)*. Let's eat instead.
  (To entice him.) We've got chunky peanut butter.

SAM. On white bread? With marshmallow Fluff?

  *(They run off to kitchen. HOUDINI suddenly sees the
  audience, preens, and plays to it grandly.)*

HOUDINI *(bowing with a flourish)*. Ladies and gentlemen.
  Perhaps my reputation precedes me. I am the Great
  Houdini. Pay no mind to that little braggart. The child
  cannot shine my spats. Frankly, he annoys me.

SAM *(offstage)*. Hey, Deed, where's the Fluff?

DARCY *(offstage)*. Look in my room.

  (SAM enters, looking for Fluff.)

HOUDINI *(unhappy)*. But, alas, he calls for me. Relent-
  lessly.

SAM. Hey, Deed? I don't see it! Deed? *(SAM exits again.)*

HOUDINI. I appear before you today to tell you a story.
  Not his, however.

*(HOUDINI magically makes a jar of Fluff appear.
DARCY enters and sees it.)*

DARCY. It was right in front of your face. *(Picks up Fluff.)*
HOUDINI. Hers. *(DARCY exits with the Fluff.)* But first,
about me. Born Erich Weiss, a poor rabbi's son, I became The Man Who Could Walk Through Walls.
Chained or shackled, roped or cuffed, I could escape
from anything made by man or God. Failure meant a
sudden, gruesome death. I never failed. How did I do it?
The know-it-alls called it a miracle. They were idiots.
The truth is, I did tricks, not miracles. For after my dear
mother died, I longed for a miracle—to enter the spirit
world while still alive, to hear her voice just once more.
But alas, even I, the Great Houdini, could not do it. Not
without a miracle.

*(DARCY and SAM enter. She chugs the last of the milk
from the carton, he finishes last bites of a sandwich.)*

SAM. Food of the gods. My home is junk-food challenged.
*(They play catch with the empty carton. As SAM man-
gles it:)* I wish this was Henry Farmer's head.
HOUDINI. And I did not believe in miracles.

(SAM throws the carton to DARCY.)

DARCY *(as she kicks it back to him)*. I wish it was Amanda
Bliss's butt!
HOUDINI. Tonight I offer you, dear people, my finest performance—dazzling storytelling, astonishing feats of
magic. At times I will even enter the story, playing various parts. All thus proving, with great humility, that I—
(shoots SAM a dirty look)—was the greatest entertainer

who ever lived. And now I give you ... the story of a miracle.

(DAVID DEETON enters and grabs the carton mid-throw.)

DAVID *(to DARCY).* Go long! *(He fires it to her like a football, she nabs it.)* Yes! David Deeton's little sister makes a circus grab in the end zone. And the fans go wild! Man, it's nice out, huh? Still feels like summer.

SAM. Global warming. Noun. An increase in the temperature of the Earth's atmosphere.

DAVID. You kill me with that stuff, Sam. *(To DARCY.)* So, you wanted me to hear some big speech you wrote?

DARCY. What if I stutter and my whole class laughs?

DAVID. No way. You'll be great.

SAM. Agreed.

DARCY. I'm only great with you guys. The rest of the time, I'm this dweeb, Stutter-girl. Here goes nothing. *(Climbs on the trunk.)* The Person I Admire Most, by Darcy Deeton, grade 6. I cried the first time I saw the ocean, because I knew my dad would make me swim in it. When I was four I fell into a swimming pool and almost drowned. Ever since then, I've been afraid of things. My dad says all it takes to get over fear is willpower. So when he ordered me to put my head under, I used all my willpower. But my mouth and lungs filled with water, it was so scary, like drowning all over again. The next thing I knew, I was lifted up, and my brother David was smiling at me, and the bad feelings went away. He said when I was ready, he'd teach me to swim, and I'd be a great swimmer. I thought how lucky I am that David is my brother, because he believes in me even when I don't believe in myself. This is why he is the person I admire most.

DAVID *(touched)*. That's awesome, Darce. You sure can write.

DARCY. But what if I stutter and they all laugh at me?

DAVID. Hey, wanna know what I do when I'm scared?

DARCY. You?

DAVID. Sure. Like, we play Oshkosh tomorrow night. They play dirty. So what do I do? I pretend they don't scare me. Pretend myself right out of the fear. Run right past 'em.

DARCY. Great. I'll remember that next time I suit up.

DAVID. You gotta believe in yourself, Darce. Then you can do anything. *(Looks at his watch.)* Oh, man, I'm late.

SAM. Got a hot date? Is it luh-luh-luh-love?

DARCY *(scoffing)*. I'm so sure.

DAVID. Tell Dad I won't be home for dinner. See ya.
(HOUDINI points at the door, which magically opens. DAVID looks at it curiously, shrugs, exits. SAM opens the trunk.)

SAM. Madam, your trunk.

DARCY. Nope.

SAM. You're afraid.

DARCY. So?

SAM. Two things overcome fear. One—you have to be highly motivated. And two—

SAM & HOUDINI. You have to believe in yourself.

DARCY. Please. That's what David says. That's what everyone says.

SAM & HOUDINI *(thundering)*. The Great Sam(Hou)-dini is not everyone!

SAM (*normal voice*). Look, there's nothing to be afraid of. Watch how fast I escape. Time me.

(*SAM gets in the trunk. DARCY locks SAM in, then crosses in front of the screen and times his escape as she speaks.*)

DARCY. Sometimes, Sam—don't tell anyone—I wish I really could become someone else. Hey, maybe this is only my larval stage and I'll turn into this beautiful butterfly girl. I'll be brave, like David. And tall. Everyone in my family is brave and tall but weird me. I hate hunting. I hate dirt bikes. Did you know I'm the only one in my family who even has a library card? Sam? Sam? (*Nothing from inside the trunk.*) Sam? (*She runs behind the screen. (Panicked.)*) Sam! Get out! Bang if you're okay! I can't get the lock open! I've gotta get help! Keep breathing!

(*DARCY runs toward the door, as SAM strolls out from behind the screen.*)

SAM (*calling to her, with a huge grin*). Miss me?

HOUDINI. Highly doubtful.

(*DARCY runs and punches him.*)

DARCY. You idiot! You really scared me.

(*As they tease and argue—*)

DOUG DEETON (*offstage, furious*). What the—I don't believe it! Who the hell...

(*DOUG DEETON enters angrily, with a bright pink leaflet and a portable phone. A back injury has him in constant pain.*)

DOUG DEETON (*punching numbers into the phone*). Didn't you hear anyone?

DARCY (*nervous*). Wh-where?

DOUG DEETON. At the front—(*The phone is answered.*) Massey? Deeton. I just got home and found that piece of filth leaflet under my own front ... right, the same one that showed up on your block. I looked down the street and saw these bright pink things sticking out of everyone's door! Thought they could sneak around and do it on Sunday morning while everyone was at church ... No, I didn't see them, but ... Fine. I'll fill out a report when I get there, I've gotten real damn good at sitting on my butt filling out reports. (*Hangs up.*)

DARCY. D-dad? W-what happened?

DOUG DEETON (*ignoring her question*). Did you do your chores yet?

DARCY. N-no, sir.

DOUG DEETON (*to SAM*). Dee Dee has chores to do, Sam. Time to go home.

SAM. My father made soy burgers for lunch. I choose chores.

DOUG DEETON (*to DARCY*). Chores. Now.

(*DOUG exits, the flyer is left on the table. SAM crosses, reads the flyer.*)

DARCY. What does it say?

SAM (*to divert her attention*). I'm still hungry. Possibly it's a tapeworm. Noun. Ribbon-like parasite that lives in the—

(*DARCY crosses, reads flyer.*)

DARCY (*reading*). "Attention Homeowners! Do you know that Appleton's maniac police officer Doug Deeton is your neighbor?"

HOUDINI. She knew what they were saying about her father. But she didn't want to think about it. So she
thought about chores instead. Every Sunday, she had
home chores, and one looming away-from-home chore,
at an ugly brick building that smelled like death. Appleton Acres Nursing Home.

*(A room in the nursing home. In bed, still, is an old
woman, Meemaw. We can't see her face.)*

HOUDINI. Room 104. Home for the last two years of Mrs.
Deanna Deeton, grandmother. Formerly a teacher of
English, currently ... *(A beat.)* Meemaw, they call her.

*(DARCY and SAM enter reluctantly and sit as far from
Meemaw as possible. SAM pulls out a deck of cards.)*

SAM. I've mastered a new trick even Houdini couldn't do.
Nothing up my sleeves. Pick a card, any card.
*(SAM fans the cards. HOUDINI flicks his finger against
them and they fly all over the bed. Meemaw doesn't re-
act.)*
DARCY. Sam! *(She and SAM cross to the bed, stare down
at Meemaw.)* It costs my parents like a hundred dollars a
day to keep her here.
SAM. For that kind of money, they should provide enter-
tainment. *(Beat.)* You think she's still in there, Deed?
DARCY. Nope. If she was in there, she'd still blink when
you asked her a question—once for yes, twice for no.
She hasn't blinked in a year now. *(They gingerly pick up
cards, then cross and sit again. DARCY checks watch.)*
Eight minutes down, fifty-two to go.

(The door opens, DAVID enters.)

DAVID. Hey, guys. What's up?

DARCY. What are you doing here?

(DAVID crosses, pulls a chair up to the bed, and takes his grandmother's hand.)

DAVID. Same thing you're doing. *(To Meemaw.)* So, you doing okay today, Meemaw? *(He waits for her to blink. Nothing happens.)* Hey, remember that test on Hamlet I told you about? I got a B. Pretty good, huh? *(He waits expectantly.)*

DARCY. Why are you talking to her when she isn't there? No one else talks to her since she stopped blinking, you know.

DAVID. Maybe she just doesn't want to blink. 'Cuz she's mad. You know, 'cuz ever since her stroke she can't do anything. But one day she'll want to tell me something so bad she won't be able to stop herself. That's when she'll blink again.

DARCY. No offense, but that's loony.

DAVID. Sometimes, Darce, when it's really quiet, I can feel her talking to me. It's…I just have faith in it, I guess.

DARCY. Definition, please.

SAM. Faith. Noun. Belief in—

DARCY *(withering)*. Not you.

DAVID *(struggling to find the right words)*. It's…when your heart tells you something is true even if you can't prove it. *(A beat.)*

DARCY. It's not like she was such a great grandmother. She could have given me a computer. But no. All she ever gave me was a map of the sky and the stars, and a stupid list of the hundred best books for young people.

DAVID. What number are you on now?

DARCY. Twenty-seven. *A Tree Grows in Brooklyn.*

DAVID. Is it good?

DARCY *(grudgingly).* Beyond.

DAVID. Did ya hear that, Meemaw? Beyond. So I wanted to tell you why I didn't show up this morning. I was with someone special. I really want you to meet her.

DARCY. Her? Who?

DAVID *(to Meemaw).* You'll like her—she's smart.

DARCY. Who's smart?

DAVID. She's so amazing. I never knew I could feel this way.

(SAM sings "You Light Up My Life" dramatically and badly.)

DARCY. Some girl? You met some girl?

DAVID & HOUDINI. Not just some girl. *The* girl.

SAM *(still singing).* You light up my days, and fill my nights...

DARCY *(to SAM).* Shut up!

DAVID. She's just so... *(To Meemaw.)* Can I bring her in to meet you?

DARCY. What?

DAVID. I know you mean yes, Meemaw. *(Crosses to the door.)*

DARCY. Now? She's here, now?

(Hand-in-hand, DAVID leads CRYSTAL EVANS into the room.)

DAVID *(with love and pride).* Meemaw, Darce, Sam, I want you to meet Crystal Evans. This is the girl I love.

HOUDINI. Now, for the first time, David's heart belonged to someone else. He spent all his time with her, Crystal. There was no time for Darcy. And it was all her fault.

(Outside of school. DARCY writes angrily. SAM enters eating a candy bar. He reads over her shoulder.)

SAM *(reading)*. "CRYSTAL EVANS stinks like SH—" *(DARCY pulls the notebook away. SAM breaks his candy bar in two and hands half to DARCY.)* I see we're lunching al fresco.

(HOUDINI dons a baseball cap, enters as HENRY FARMER, bully, with AMANDA BLISS, cruel.)

HENRY-HOUDINI *(gets idea for cruel joke, imitates teacher in falsetto)*. Time for attendance, class! Henry Farmer? *(Deep voice.)* Here. *(Falsetto.)* Amanda Bliss?
AMANDA. Here!
HENRY-HOUDINI. Stuh-Stuh-Stutter-girl? Shrimp-boy?
AMANDA. The cootie couple! Aren't you gonna say "here"?
SAM *(to DARCY)*. Abscond. Verb. Go away secretly. Shall we?
(SAM and DARCY start to leave, but HENRY-HOUDINI bumps into SAM on purpose.)
HENRY-HOUDINI. Hey, watch it, Shrimp-boy! *(HENRY looms over SAM.)*
SAM *(beat)*. I've decided to let you go this time. Just don't let it happen again.
HENRY-HOUDINI *(laughing)*. You're a weenie, Samdini!
AMANDA. Hey, do a trick and make yourself grow so you can kiss Stuh-Stuh-Stutter-girl!

(HENRY and AMANDA exit laughing. HOUDINI removes HENRY FARMER hat.)

HOUDINI. For Darcy, the ignobilities of both school and home continued, despite the approach of her twelfth birthday.

(DARCY's room. She is writing.)

DARCY *(reading aloud as she writes).* "Secret Solemn Vows on My Twelfth Birthday. One: grow breasts. Two: stop stuttering. Three, most important of all: stop being afraid."

(She puts the paper in her pocket. The dining room. CLAIRE DEETON, Darcy's mom, sets the table for her birthday party, DOUG awkwardly wraps DARCY's gift, a sweater.)

DOUG DEETON. Do you know who that lying scum wife-beater Hunter hired to defend him? Gold and Barrick. The rich defending the rich. It makes me sick.

CLAIRE DEETON. The lawyers are just doing their job. At least the D.A. upped the charges to a felony.

DOUG DEETON. Yeah? Who's gonna testify? Hunter's wife? She calls 911, I show up to find the drunk sonuv-abitch beating her up, I go to arrest him, he pushes me down the stairs and wrecks my back, but I get up and save her butt anyway. So then what does she do? She goes back to him. And they sue me!

CLAIRE DEETON. Doug—

DOUG DEETON. Undue use of force. Me!

CLAIRE DEETON. No one who really knows you could ever believe it.

DOUG DEETON. Tell that to every bleeding heart in Wisconsin. Hunter's connected. No way he Hunter beats his wife. Hell, there's a photo in the paper of him and his wife at some charity thing. Deeton? Just some dumb-ass cop with a chip on his shoulder trying to stick it to a rich guy. *(About his gift-wrapping.)* I can't wrap this sweater.

CLAIRE DEETON *(tenderly)*. You're doing fine.

DOUG DEETON. A sweater. She wants a computer so bad.

CLAIRE DEETON. Maybe next year.

DOUG DEETON. That's what we told her last year, when I thought I'd get a promotion. Of course I didn't know that Hunter was gonna wreck my back and put me on permanent desk duty. Which means no promotion, ever, probably. And no computer.

CLAIRE DEETON. I can ask for more overtime—

DOUG DEETON *(wounded pride)*. You think that's what I want?

CLAIRE DEETON. No.

DOUG DEETON. Hunter probably has a computer in every room of his house. Color-coordinated by his decorator or something. Musta been hard-pressed to figure out which one to use to print those damn leaflets. *(Beat.)* Dee Dee saw it. It's not right. Damn them, anyway.

CLAIRE DEETON *(sadly)*. It used to make you so mad, cops who talk the way you're talking now. You said you'd never be like them.

DOUG DEETON. I was an idiot.

CLAIRE DEETON *(wistfully)*. No. You were my hero.

(She goes to embrace him as SAM enters, hair slicked, wearing a sports jacket and carrying a wrapped gift.)

CLAIRE DEETON. Sam! Don't you look nice. You can put that on the table.

(She exits into kitchen. DARCY runs in.)

DARCY. I thought I heard Davi—*(Sees SAM.)* Oh. It's you. *(DARCY notices SAM's slicked hair and sports jacket.)* Why do you look like that?

SAM. Genetics. Sadly, it's out of my hands.

HOUDINI. Just when she was sure David had forgotten her birthday, in he walked, carrying a small wrapped gift.

DOUG, CLAIRE, DAVID & SAM *(singing last line)*. "Happy Birthday dear Dee Dee, Happy Birthday to you!" *(DARCY blows out the candles on her cake, everyone claps.)*

DOUG DEETON *(awkwardly nice)*. You're getting mighty big, birthday girl.

DARCY. Am not. I'm as runty as ever.

CLAIRE DEETON. Don't worry, sweetie. I didn't grow until seventh grade.

DOUG DEETON. And I fell in love with her in sixth.

DARCY *(been there, done that)*. And by the time you were seniors, you were engaged. I've heard that story a zillion times. *(To CLAIRE.)* I want the most gigunda piece of cake!

(As she reaches for it, the paper with her secret vows falls from her pocket. DOUG picks it up, reads it.)

DOUG *(teasing)*. Ho, what's this? Number one, grow breasts—

DARCY *(panicked)*. Give me that!

CLAIRE. Watch the milk!

(DARCY lunges for the paper, spilling milk onto DOUG. He jumps up without thinking.)

DOUG. For crying out—*(He gasps in pain. His back.)*

CLAIRE. What?

DOUG *(in agony)*. Spasm.

CLAIRE. I'll get your pills—

DOUG. I don't want a—

DAVID *(hurrying to him)*. Let me help you to bed, Dad.

DOUG. And I don't want to go to bed! I'm not a damn invalid! *(Turning anger on DARCY.)* Can't you do anything right?

(DARCY bolts, humiliated.)

DAVID. Darce! *(To his parents.)* I'll go.

(DAVID goes after her. DARCY's bedroom.)

DARCY *(to DAVID)*. Why does he hate me?

DAVID. He doesn't.

DARCY. Ever since he got hurt, he yells at me all the time.

DAVID. It's not you, Darce. It's his back. And the lawsuit. And money. And—

DARCY. But I didn't do any of that.

DAVID. Yeah, I know. You want some tissues? *(HOUDINI magically makes tissues appear near DAVID, who hands some to DARCY.)* Better?

DARCY *(nods, then halting)*. You don't think...I mean, Dad gets so mad. He didn't hurt Mr. Hunter on purpose. Did he?

DAVID. No way.

DARCY. But how do you know?

DAVID. I just do. The same way I know Dad loves you.

DARCY. I wish I did.

DAVID. Look, I know it's not right that he takes stuff out on you, Darce. And it's so weird, because Meemaw used to take stuff out on him, remember? But I always knew, deep down, that she loved him. Just like I know that he loves you.

DARCY *(dubious)*. You have faith, I suppose.

DAVID. Yeah, birthday girl. In you.

HOUDINI. They returned to the scene of the crime. Her father had gone to bed. She opened her presents, saving David's for last.

(The dining room. CLAIRE, SAM, DAVID and DARCY, surrounded by gifts and torn wrapping paper. DAVID hands DARCY his gift.)

DARCY *(excited, about to tear it open)*. What is it?

(The doorbell rings.)

DAVID. I'll get it. *(He exits eagerly.)*

SAM *(to DARCY)*. Foreboding. Adjective. Uninvited dread.

(DAVID returns with CRYSTAL, who holds a wrapped gift.)

DAVID *(too hearty)*. Look who's here!

SAM. It's Uninvited Dread!

CLAIRE. What a nice surprise.

CRYSTAL. Thanks, Mrs. Deeton. *(To DARCY.)* I hope you don't mind that Davie invited me to crash your party, Darce.

DARCY *(coldly)*. Don't call me Darce. Davie is the only one who calls me that.

CRYSTAL. Oh, sorry. (*Holds out gift to DARCY.*) Happy birthday. (*DARCY reluctantly opens her present, a hardcover book.*) *The Member of the Wedding,* by Carson McCullers. Number twenty-eight on your list, isn't it? That's what Davie told me.

DARCY (*flat*). It's very nice. Thank you.

DAVID. Open mine, now.

(*She opens it; a heart-shaped locket. DAVID puts it around DARCY's neck.*)

CLAIRE. Oh, Dee Dee, that's beautiful.

DAVID. Like it?

DARCY. I love it. I'm going to wear it all the time.

CLAIRE. Go show your father, sweetie.

DARCY (*so happy*). I will!

(*Before DARCY can exit, CRYSTAL reaches into her own neckline and pulls out an identical necklace.*)

CRYSTAL. And look, Dee Dee! Davie got me the exact same necklace. Isn't that sweet? It's almost like we're sisters!

DARCY. I don't want a sister. And if I did, it wouldn't be you.

CLAIRE DEETON. Darcy! Apologize this instant.

DARCY. No. You can't make me.

CRYSTAL. It's okay, Mrs. Dee—

CLAIRE DEETON. It is not okay. She's impossible.

DARCY. Good. I want to be impossible.

HOUDINI. Thus ended the festivities. Sam went home. David and that girl left for a concert in the park. And Darcy went to bed. But when she woke up an hour later, something inside her had changed.

(*DARCY's bedroom. She writes in her journal.*

DARCY (*reads aloud as she writes*). "New and Improved Secret Solemn Vows on My Twelfth Birthday. One: be more mature. Two: apologize to David and her. Three: try to mean it."

HOUDINI. She snuck out of the house, into the cold night air, hurrying toward Appleton Square Park. She searched the crowd for David and her. Nothing. And then, at last, she saw them.

(*The park. DAVID and CRYSTAL on a park bench, embracing. DARCY hides in the shadows. CRYSTAL holds up her necklace.*)

CRYSTAL. I love this so much.

DAVID. I guess that means you've got my heart.

CRYSTAL. I'm so glad I talked you into getting Darcy one, too.

DAVID. Not that she appreciated it. She's been a real brat lately.

CRYSTAL. This is hard on her, Davie. She worships you. She wants to be with you all the time.

DAVID (*groaning*). Believe me, I know. So let's take advantage of the fact that she's not here now.

(*They kiss. DARCY steps out of shadows.*)

CRYSTAL (*sees DARCY, startled*). Darce!

DAVID. What are you doing here?

DARCY (*furious*). I came here to apologize. And what did I find out? The necklace wasn't even your idea. It was her idea.

DAVID (*exasperated*). What difference does it make?

DARCY. I hate her.

DAVID. Darce, come on, you don't mean it—

DARCY. I do mean it. I hate her g-guts. And I hate your guts, too. I wish you were *dead*.
(*She tears off the necklace and throws it at him, then runs off. DAVID runs after her.*)

DAVID. Darce. Darce!

HOUDINI. She could hear him running after her, calling her—

DAVID (*offstage*). —Come on, Darce!

HOUDINI. She ran ever faster. He would never catch her, she would run out of her own skin, become someone else, anyone else. She darted between two parked cars. He ran after her.

DAVID (*offstage*). Darce! I—
(*Sound: a car skidding, an impact. Add spot on DARCY, panting, wild-eyed.*)

HOUDINI. Oh my God, he ran right in front of that car.

DARCY. If I don't turn around, it won't be true—

HOUDINI. Is he dead?

DARCY. Please, God, make it not be true.

HOUDINI. I'll call 911,

DARCY (*falls to her knees, a terrible cry*). DAVID!

(*Blackout. Sound: a siren, a beating heart. CRYSTAL enters with a lit candle, someone joins her, then many, each with lit candles. Spot up on DR. LEE. Her lines and DARCY's overlap here.*)

DR. LEE. I'm Dr. Stacey Lee. I'd like to read a statement. At six this morning, life support was removed from David Deeton.

(Add spot on DARCY, downstage.)

DARCY *(petrified)*. I told you before, I was in the park.
  B-but I didn't see wh-what happened.
DR. LEE. David was carrying an organ donor card and his
  parents have honored his wishes.
DARCY. I d-didn't see anything.
DR. LEE. I want to tell all those who are mourning today,
  that David Deeton died a hero.
DARCY. I don't know what happened. I don't know!
  (The candles all go out.)
HOUDINI. On the walls, David's photos. On the mantle,
  his trophies. He was everywhere, but nowhere.

(DARCY's bedroom. She reads from her journal.)

DARCY *(reading what she's written)*. "The man driving
  the car that hit David was rich. The police said it was an
  accident. My father says rich people think they are
  above the law and it was the rich man's fault. But it was
  not."

*(Add DEETON's living room. CLAIRE and DOUG sit,
numb.)*

DOUG DEETON *(flat, to CLAIRE)*. What time is it?
CLAIRE DEETON *(flat, to DOUG)*. I don't know. Late.
DARCY. I'm the only one who knows whose fault it really
  was.
CLAIRE DEETON. We should go to bed. *(They don't move.)*
DARCY. It's been two months now. No one talks about it.
  At night I'm afraid to sleep because I hear the walls of

our house whispering to me. So instead of sleeping, I stare out at the stars, and listen to myself breathe, in, out, in, out.

DOUG DEETON. We should go to bed. *(They don't move.)*

DARCY. And I think: if I stop doing this, I will die. But I would rather die, than tell what the walls are whispering.

HOUDINI *(whispered)*. "Murderer."

(A burst of convivial group laughter, good cheer. Front hall of WEISS's home. AARON WEISS enters.)

AARON WEISS *(calling back to his company)*. Ha! You laugh, but wait 'til you taste my pies—no white sugar, no white flour, and—

(DARCY enters.)

AARON WEISS *(surprised)*. Dee Dee! Happy Thanksgiving! How are you?

DARCY. Is Sam here? *(More laughter, good cheer.)* I guess you're having Thanksgiving dinner. I should go.

AARON WEISS. No, no, don't leave. I'll get Sam. Or come in and join us for dessert. *(Beat.)* I'm so sorry about your brother.

DARCY. No you're not. You're a lawyer.

AARON WEISS. Lawyers care too, Darcy.

DARCY. My father says lawyers don't care if the person they defend is guilty or innocent. All they care about is winning and making money.

AARON WEISS. Dee Dee—

DARCY. I have to go. I shouldn't have come here. *(She crosses outside, stands alone.)* Why I Wish I Could Fly, by Darcy Deeton.

(SAM comes out after her, no coat. They look at each other. A beat.)

DARCY. Only a moron would come outside without a jacket when it's this cold, Sam.

SAM *(shivering).* I was highly motivated.

DARCY. My father doesn't want me to come over here anymore.

SAM. But you came anyway. Duly noted. *(Beat.)* I dream about David sometimes.

DARCY *(giving SAM her scarf).* I don't.

SAM *(beat).* Inspiration! Noun. A sudden brilliant idea. I ask Houdini to help us commune with David's spirit, so you can talk to him.

DARCY. No one can do that.

SAM. What if you're wrong?

DARCY. I'm not. I'm never going to get to talk to David again. My life will just go on and on because I'm too chicken to stop breathing, and I'll never get to tell him I didn't mean to—

SAM. Mean to what?

DARCY *(beat).* I wish I was dead. *(SAM awkwardly holds her. A beat.)* This does not count as our first date. OK?

SAM. K-O. So. I felt your heart beating, ergo your petition to die has been denied. So what we need is—

DARCY *(a sudden realization).* My heart is beating.

SAM. Affirmative. Perhaps if—

DARCY. My heart is beating. If your heart is still beating, you can't be dead. Don't you see, Sam? Someone else's heart is still beating, too. *(Beat.)* I have to do it. We have to. Find David's heart. Sam?

SAM *(a beat, then he smiles at her)*. K-O.

HOUDINI. They searched the Internet every day for David's heart. And searched. And searched. It was only days before Christmas now.

(SAM's room. DARCY uses SAM's computer. SAM tries on sunglasses, admiring himself in the mirror.)

DARCY *(so tired)*. I'm searching Yahoo! again for heart transplants.

SAM *(suavely to his reflection)*. The name is Bond. James Bond.

DARCY. I'll try "waiting list" again, too.

SAM *(changes sunglasses; to reflection as Elvis)*. Thankyu, Thank-yu very much.

DARCY. Are you going to help me or are you going to try on your Chanukah presents?

SAM. Do these make me look taller?

DARCY *(weary)*. Forget it. It says recipient information is confidential. That's what it always says.

(AARON WEISS enters.)

AARON WEISS. Where's your Hebrew book, Sam? You're supposed to be studying for your bar mitzvah.

SAM. The Great Samdini is taking a well-deserved break.

AARON WEISS. Well, the Father of the Great Samdini says break time is over. I've got a meeting. When I get back, you and I are working on your Hebrew. *(HOUDINI magically makes a Hebrew book appear. AARON sees it and hands it to SAM. To DARCY, gently:)* I'm not your enemy, Dee Dee. *(He exits.)*

SAM *(an idea hits)*. I'm *so* dense.

DARCY. He is too my enemy.

SAM. Newspaper. Newspaper search, Deed.

DARCY *(bitter)*. I lie to my father just so I can come over—

SAM. Don't you get it? We can find David's heart! *(SAM hurries to his computer. As he types:)* "Search Nexus national newspaper database for the following words and phrases in the same article: September 25. Heart transplant. High school athlete. Wisconsin." *(He punches a final button. Tense, they watch the screen.)*

HOUDINI. Like magic, the screen filled.

DARCY. Oh, my God, it worked. *The Miami Herald.* September 25th.

DARCY & SAM *(reading)*. "MIAMI YOUTH GETS NEW HEART. Miami Beach youth Winston Pawling, 12, received a heart transplant yesterday at the University of Pittsburgh Medical Center."

DARCY *(stops reading)*. A kid. I never thought—

SAM. Me, neither. *(Reading.)* "A high school athlete in Wisconsin, fatally injured when hit by a car, was the donor. Pawling is the son of Miami doctors John-Paul and Linda Pawling. He was reported in good condition after his surgery."

DARCY. You know what we have to do, don't you?

SAM. Miami, huh? What luck. I can use my new sunglasses.

DARCY. I only have twenty-four dollars in my piggy bank.

SAM. It so happens I'm flush at the moment. Chanukah gelt. My grandma gives cash.

DARCY. We'll leave in the morning. We can take my bike to the library and walk to the bus depot. Tell your dad you'll be with me so he won't look for you. *(Beat.)* I'll pay you back some day, Sam. I promise.

SAM *(Samdini voice)*. The Great Samdini cares not about money. Consider it a gift.

DARCY. Some gifts are worth more than all the money in the world, Sam. Thank you.

SAM *(sincere)*. You're welcome.

HOUDINI. Her head was full of plans that night, as she tiptoed into her dark, silent house, that was no longer a home. But soon, she would fly away.

(DEETON living room, barely lit by moonlight. DOUG sits, an open box at his feet, a small football in his hands. DARCY enters. She doesn't see him.)

DOUG DEETON *(eerily)*. It's almost Christmas.

DARCY *(startled)*. Dad?

DOUG DEETON. We don't have a tree. Last year we had a big tree, remember? This football was on top. "D. DEE-TON, #17," it says—I forget who made it for us.

DARCY *(nervous)*. Wh-why are you sitting in the dark, Dad?

DOUG DEETON *(picks up a ceramic angel)*. Remember this? Meemaw gave it to us. I always hated it.

DARCY *(guiltily, a confession)*. I went to Sam's.

DOUG DEETON. I really wanted to get you a computer, but I just couldn't swing it. Meemaw never got me what

I wanted for Christmas. I always vowed I wouldn't be like that with my kids. Kid.

DARCY. I'm sorry.

DOUG DEETON. You're so much like Meemaw, did I ever tell you that? She didn't want me to be a cop. Not intellectual enough for her. But a cop is all I ever wanted to be.

DARCY *(more nervous)*. You can ground me if you want.

DOUG DEETON. I wanted her to be proud of me so bad. But she never was.

DARCY. Or yell at me. You could yell at me.

DOUG DEETON. I always thought: "Deeton, if you're a good guy who plays by the rules, you'll do okay. You might not be the best or the brightest, but you'll do okay." *(A bitter laugh.)* The really funny thing is, all of it—Meemaw, my back, even getting called a racist pig— it's nothing—nothing—compared to this: I had a son. He was the best and the brightest. I was a good father. And I'd give my life for just one more day with him.

(He weeps. DARCY is frozen.)

DARCY *(to herself)*. Breathe: in, out, in out. This is how you stay alive.

(Sound: a beating heart.)

END OF ACT ONE

ACT TWO

AT RISE: *Early the next morning. DARCY's bedroom. She reads a letter she's written. HOUDINI is present and lost in his own thoughts. All lines overlap slightly, dreamlike.*

DARCY. Dear Mom and Dad, By the time you get this I'll be gone. I wanted you to know why I have to leave...

HOUDINI. Dearest Momma, Why did you have to leave me? From the day of your death to the day of my own, I searched for you...

DARCY. When I was little, Meemaw taught me the names of stars...

HOUDINI. Where were you?

DARCY. My favorite is Betelgeuse. It glows bright red, and it's five hundred and twenty-seven light years from Earth. If Betelgeuse died tonight, its light would still shine for another five hundred and twenty-seven years...

HOUDINI. To hear your voice just once more became my dearest wish—

DARCY. I wish it was like that when someone you love dies, but it isn't. Their light goes out right away, and you can't fool yourself into thinking they still exist, like you can with a star...

HOUDINI. Psychics and mediums swore to me that they could reach you, that they could bring your voice to me ...

DARCY. But if a person's heart is still beating, then their light is still shining. That's why I have to find David's heart ...

HOUDINI. They were all fakes. Frauds!

DARCY. When I said I didn't see what happened that night, I lied.

HOUDINI. Liars. They broke my heart ...

DARCY. The truth is ... *(She falters.)*

HOUDINI *(sadly).* They did tricks. Just like me.

DARCY. The truth is ...

DARCY & HOUDINI. The truth is ...

(DARCY tears up the letter and stuffs the shreds into her backpack. Next morning. A moving bus. DARCY and SAM sit across from ENID MANNERS, a gullible woman. HOUDINI dons a cap, becomes the BUS DRIVER.)

BUS DRIVER-HOUDINI *(over hand-held PA).* Good morning, folks, this bus is bound for Miami, Florida. Now sit back, relax, and enjoy the trip. Merry Christmas, folks.

DARCY. We're really doing it.

SAM *(both proud and nervous).* Take that, Henry Farmer.

DARCY *(ditto).* Eat dirt and die, Amanda Bliss!

SAM *(beat).* Everyone will be looking for us, you know.

DARCY. By the time they realize we're gone, we'll be far, far away. *(She takes out a book.)*

SAM *(incredulously reading the title). The Member of the Wedding.* You packed the book Crystal gave you?

DARCY. I'm weird. *(Reading aloud.)* "It happened that green and crazy summer when Frankie was twelve years

old. This was the summer when for a long time she had
not been a member." *(SAM yawns, closes his eyes.)*
"She belonged to no club and was a member of nothing
in the world." *(Awed.)* Nothing in the world.

HOUDINI. The bus rolled south. Milwaukee; Chicago; Gary,
Indiana; she didn't care; she read on.

*(Lights change indicating passage of time as DARCY
reads. She nudges SAM awake.)*

DARCY *(so excited)*. This book—this girl, Frankie, is
crazy about her older brother, only he's getting married,
and she's so afraid that now she'll be all alone—

SAM *(groggily)*. Uh-huh. Where are we?

DARCY. An "I" instead of a "we." "The we of me." Isn't
that so perfect, Sam? "The we of me."

ENID *(timidly leans over)*. Hello. I hope I'm not intruding.
Are you children going home for Christmas?

DARCY *(sotto to SAM)*. Lie.

SAM *(totally making it up as he goes along)*. Yep. We're
heading home. To...Granny! We live with her. Because
our dysfunctional parents are...traveling with the circus.

ENID *(concerned)*. Oh, my.

DARCY *(to get SAM to shut up)*. She isn't interested.

ENID. Oh, but I am!

SAM *(smug, to DARCY)*. Oh, but she is. *(To ENID.)* I have
my own circus act. Perhaps my reputation precedes me.
The Great Samdini—greatest magician and escape artist
who ever lived?

ENID. My. You're young to be so successful.

SAM. Prodigy. Noun. Me.

DARCY. Moron. Noun. You.

SAM (*grandly indicating DARCY*). She's my lowly—
(*DARCY pokes him.*) Lovely ... lowly assistant.

ENID. I'm Enid Manners. Please call me Enid.

SAM. Sam—(*DARCY pokes SAM harder, a reminder not
to give his name. He blurts first thing that comes into his
mind.*)—Monella!

ENID. Salmonella, did you say? Isn't that food poisoning,
dear?

SAM (*thinking fast, still making it up as he goes*). Ah yes.
So confusing. Actually, it's Sam-Dean Monella. That's
where I got my stage name—Samdini. This is my sister ... Amanda-Bliss Monella. But surely you've heard of
our parents, Patella and Rubella Monella, the Fabulous
Flying Monellas?

HOUDINI. Enid had never heard of the Fabulous Flying
Monellas, so Sam regaled her with stories about his life
in show business, all of which he stole from my life.
Many blatant lies later, the bus driver pulled off the
highway, in the booming metropolis of—

(*HOUDINI dons BUS DRIVER cap.*)

BUS DRIVER-HOUDINI. Clarksville, Tennessee, folks.
This will be your basic one-hour dinner stop, folks.

(*Night. Carnival sounds. Outside the bus. SAM, DARCY
and ENID without jackets.*)

SAM. Wow, it's warm here. (*Pointing.*) Hey, Deed, look!

DARCY (*reading a large sign*). "CLARKSVILLE WINTER
CARNIVAL."

ENID (*wistfully*). Oh my, doesn't that look like fun?

SAM (*donning sunglasses, à la Elvis*). Pretty mamas, we are so over there already.

ENID (*hesitating*). I'm afraid my funds are rather limited.

DARCY (*linking arms with ENID*). Come on.

HOUDINI. It was glorious—cotton candy, the merry-go-round, the toy horse race. After watching three boys in a row lose, Darcy tried her arm at Toss-the-Football-Through-the-Tire.

(*The carnival. DARCY has won a giant stuffed bunny. Our trio is in high spirits. NOTE: all actors not in carnival scenes serve as THE CROWD.*)

ENID. You certainly can throw a football, Amanda-Bliss!

(*As they walk through carnival, HOUDINI dons various hats or wigs, instantly changing character—SANTA, RAFFLE LADY, DONKEY MAN.*)

SANTA-HOUDINI. Ho, ho, ho, Merry Christmas! (*To SAM.*) And Happy Chanukah!

RAFFLE LADY-HOUDINI. Raffle tickets, kids? I've still got five hundred left to sell.

ENID (*eagerly, to DARCY and SAM*). What next?

DONKEY MAN-HOUDINI (*Irish*). Give the wee ones a ride on Daisy the Docile Donkey!

DARCY. Let's go on the Ferris wheel, okay?

RAFFLE LADY-HOUDINI. How about one raffle ticket, then? Just one?

SAM (*to DARCY*). K-O.

(Add lights on AMAZIN' EDDIE, escape artist, on stage with a trunk and a microphone.)

AMAZIN' EDDIE *(into mike)*. Come one and all to see me, Amazin' Eddie, World's Greatest Escape Artist! Better than Houdini!

SAM *(offended)*. That guy isn't better than Houdini.

HOUDINI. Precisely!

SAM. I'm the only one better than Houdini.

HOUDINI *(dryly)*. We press on. Enid said she'd meet them on the bus. Before she left, Darcy managed to slip some money into Enid's purse. Sam and Darcy hurried to the wheel, bought tickets, then climbed into the rocking seats. Whoosh—up, around, flying, free! Below, a quilt of carnival colors. Above, a blanket of stars.

(Music. The platform has become the Ferris wheel. SAM and DARCY are mid-ride.)

DARCY *(joyfully)*. Look, there's Betelgeuse! Right there! I never want to get off, Sam. Let's stay on forever.

SAM. I could do my bar mitzvah up here. Upside down. In a straitjacket!

(The music slows and the wheel stops, with them at the top.)

DARCY *(guilt floods her)*. We stopped. *(Beat.)* It's over.

SAM. I feel tall up here. Like I could touch the stars. *(Beat.)* When did you feel the very best about yourself, Deed?

DARCY. Dunno.

SAM. You remember in fourth grade, when Henry Farmer called me Shrimp-boy for the zillionth time and I finally kicked him?

DARCY. And he gave you a bloody nose and you got suspended? That's when you felt the best about yourself?

SAM. It's the only time in my whole life I wasn't a coward.

DARCY (*looking down at the ground*). Uh, Sam? (*They both look down.*)

SAM. The lever does not appear to be working.

DARCY (*calling*). HEY! YOU! WE HAVE TO GET DOWN! RIGHT NOW!

SAM. In what universe is that helpful? (*Points across the street.*) Enid just boarded our bus. Which leaves in precisely ... (*checks watch*) ... one minute.

DARCY. She won't let them leave without us.

(*The bus pulls out in a diesel roar.*)

SAM. This is not good.

DARCY. Okay. We're not panicking. We've got the rest of your money. We'll buy new bus tickets.

SAM (*embarrassed*). It seems I didn't want the money to fall out of my pocket, so I put it in my back—

DARCY (*panicking*). Backpack? On the bus?

SAM. We still have your money.

DARCY. It seems I slipped some of it to Enid. (*Defensive.*) Quit looking at me like that. She's poor.

SAM. How much have you got left, exactly?

DARCY. Exactly a lot!

HOUDINI. Thirty minutes later, the wheel was fixed, setting them down on terra firma once again.

(*The carnival. HOUDINI dons DONKEY MAN hat.*)

DONKEY MAN-HOUDINI *(Irish).* Let the wee ones ride on Daisy the Docile Donkey!

RAFFLE LADY-HOUDINI *(desperate).* Please, buy a raffle ticket. Someone? Anyone?

(DARCY and SAM enter, numb.)

DARCY *(shellshocked).* Six dollars. We only have six dollars.

DONKEY MAN-HOUDINI *(to SAM and DARCY).* What about a donkey ride, then, kiddies?

SAM. Thank you, but we already feel like jackasses.

(SAM and DARCY trudge on. They near AMAZIN' EDDIE's stage.)

AMAZIN' EDDIE. Ladies and gentlemen, children of all ages, I am about to perform Houdini's most amazing feat—Metamorphing!

SAM *(muttering, irritated).* Metamorphosis.

AMAZIN' EDDIE. The lovely Charlene will assist me with Metamorphing.

SAM *(more irritated).* Metamorphosis.

(CHARLENE joins EDDIE.)

AMAZIN' EDDIE. But first, I need a volunteer from the audience. You, sir.

(He points to HOUDINI, who has changed hats to become MAN IN THE CROWD. Oh-so-earnest, MAN IN

THE CROWD bounds easily up on stage. CHARLENE hands him EDDIE's handcuffs.)

AMAZIN' EDDIE. Sir, please try your hardest to open those handcuffs.

MAN IN THE CROWD-HOUDINI *(pulls on cuffs dramatically)*. Huh. Can't budge 'em.

AMAZIN' EDDIE. And please examine the lock on my trunk, sir. Surely a he-man such as yourself should be able to break that lock.

MAN IN THE CROWD-HOUDINI *(pulls lock, very exaggerated effort)*. Just can't do it.

AMAZIN' EDDIE. Thank you, sir. You may step down. And now, I, Amazin' Eddie, present ... Metamorphing.

SAM & HOUDINI *(can't take it anymore)*. METAMORPHOSIS, YOU SCHMUCK!

(SAM and HOUDINI trade curious looks, as CHARLENE puts on music and handcuffs EDDIE. He gets in trunk. She locks and ropes it shut, then pulls the screen in front of it.)

CHARLENE. Say the magic words: MERRY CHRISTMAS!

THE CROWD. MERRY CHRISTMAS!

(CHARLENE pulls screen back. EDDIE stands there, handcuffs dangle from one wrist, the trunk still locked and roped shut. He and CHARLENE bow, the crowd applauds. CHARLENE goes into crowd with hat, people stuff money in it.)

SAM *(incensed, to DARCY)*. He deeply sucks.

DARCY. Forget it, Sam. We have to—

(SAM dons sunglasses, makes his way to edge of stage.)

SAM (*gushes innocence, to EDDIE*). Gosh, Mr. Amazin', how come you only did half of the trick? And it's called Metamorphosis.

AMAZIN' EDDIE. Go change your diaper, runt.

SAM (*grabs EDDIE's handcuffs*). How do these work, Mr. Amazin'?

AMAZIN' EDDIE. Put 'em down, ya little dork!
(*EDDIE pushes SAM hard, SAM falls, his sunglasses land on stage. DARCY helps SAM up.*)

MAN IN THE CROWD-HOUDINI. Hey now, that boy is a lot smaller than you, fella.

AMAZIN' EDDIE. It was an accident, sir. (*To SAM.*) You okay, kid? (*EDDIE accidentally-on-purpose steps on SAM's sunglasses.*) Gosh, I'm sorry.

SAM (*covering humiliation*). A true Neanderthal. Possibly pre-Neanderthal. Which makes him a Homo Erectus.
(*With a hat full of money, CHARLENE rejoins EDDIE. DARCY eyes the money in the hat, and an idea dawns on her.*)

AMAZIN' EDDIE. You're a great audience, folks. The next show starts in—

DARCY. Hey, Eddie! My friend here says your act stinks like puke.

SAM. I'm dead! (*A headline.*) "Jewish Kid Murdered by Homo Erectus!"

AMAZIN' EDDIE. Hey! What'd you just say? Called me a homo with a what?

SAM (*placating*). Just a slight misunderstanding, Mr. Amazin' sir! (*To DARCY.*) This would be an excellent time to—

DARCY. Hey, Pukey-Eddie!

SAM. —Leave.

DARCY. I'll bet you fifty bucks my friend can do that trick better than you.

AMAZIN' EDDIE. Get outta my face.

SAM. Excellent concept.

MAN IN THE CROWD-HOUDINI. Scared to take a bet off a little kid, Eddie?

AMAZIN' EDDIE. I ain't afraid of jack, buddy. *(To DARCY.)* It's a bet.

DARCY. Ha! My friend's gonna kick your butt.

SAM *(to DARCY)*. Suicidal. Adjective. Good-bye. *(SAM tries to leave.)*

DARCY *(stopping him)*. Sam, don't you get it? If you do the trick as good as he did, he'll look like an idiot. Everyone will stuff that hat with money for us. Money gets us to Florida!

SAM *(a beat, real voice)*. Uh...the Great Samdini has never actually performed the real Metamorphosis in public.

DARCY. You can do it, Sam.

SAM. And the real Metamorphosis takes two people.

DARCY *(beat, fear hits her)*. No.

SAM. Yes. You got us into this.

DARCY. I c-can't. I can't! *(She hurries away, SAM follows.)*

EDDIE *(calling, smugly)*. Adios, Jew-boy!

(DARCY and SAM stop in their tracks. It's the last straw. They look at each other.)

DARCY *(to SAM, deadly serious)*. Let's do it.

(DARCY and SAM climb onto the stage. SAM crosses to mike.)

SAM *(petrified)*. Ladies and gentlemen, I am the Great Samdini. This is my assist...my partner, the Fabulous Flying Dee Dee Demento. We now present—

DARCY *(interrupting)*. One minute, please. *(She pulls SAM aside.)*

SAM *(sotto)*. What? You're wrecking the act.

DARCY *(sotto)*. I changed my mind. I can't do it.

SAM *(sotto)*. You have to do it.

DARCY *(sotto)*. I c-can't! The b-box—

EDDIE *(calling)*. Now or never, dweebs!

(SAM crosses back to the mike.)

SAM. We now present...the real Metamorphosis!

(HOUDINI points at tape deck, music. DARCY cuffs SAM, locks and ropes the trunk, pulls the screen. Panicked, she goes behind the screen. Three long beats. SAM moves the screen. DARCY's now in the trunk, yet the trunk is still locked and roped shut. SAM opens the trunk, DARCY stands, triumphant, as the audience cheers. A livid EDDIE drops fifty bucks in the hat. The CROWD adds more money as SAM and DARCY bow.)

AMAZIN' EDDIE *(reaching for hat)*. Since this is my show, this belongs to—*(DARCY grabs the hat, she and SAM run. EDDIE gives chase, calling:)* Hey, that's my hat, Jew-boy!

(MAN IN THE CROWD-HOUDINI neatly trips EDDIE as DARCY and SAM run off.)

HOUDINI *(to audience)*. An accident. Compliments of another Jew-boy. Where was I? *(A beat.)* Ah, yes. They dashed back to the bus depot, only to find it swarming with police. With nowhere to go, they ran back to the carnival. Now the booths were closing, the rides going dark. No bright lights. No music. Everything seemed to signal: the end.

(The carnival, near a horse trailer in which we see the hind end of Daisy the Donkey. DARCY and SAM enter, cold, exhausted. SAM collapses on a bench.)

SAM. Just remember, when they arrest us we get one phone call.

DARCY. We need a plan.

(HOUDINI dons DONKEY MAN hat and pats Daisy's hind end.)

DONKEY MAN-HOUDINI. Good girl, Daisy. I'll just be gettin' me pay, and then we're off to the Sunshine State. *(DONKEY MAN-HOUDINI exits. DARCY stares at Daisy, gets an idea, crosses to SAM.)*

DARCY *(furtive)*. Sam! Wake up. *(She pulls him to horse trailer.)*

SAM *(mumbling sleepily)*. Let-me-sleep-five-more-minutes-Dad-I-have-a-sore-throat-I-don't-think-I-should-go-to-scho—

DARCY. Get in.

SAM *(looks at Daisy)*. Surely you jest.

(DONKEY MAN-HOUDINI slowly backs onto the stage, waving.)

DONKEY MAN-HOUDINI. Pleasure doing business with you. Me and Daisy'll be seein' ya at next year's carnival!

(DARCY pushes SAM into the trailer, scrambling in after him. They hide under some hay. DONKEY MAN-HOU-DINI crosses toward the unseen front of his truck.)

DONKEY MAN-HOUDINI. Okay, Daisy-me-beauty, we're hitting the road.

(Sound: a truck starting. SAM and DARCY crawl out from under the hay. They sit, petrified, directly under Daisy's tail.)

DARCY *(afraid to move a muscle)*. We're moving.

SAM. Moving is good.

DARCY *(croons)*. Hi, Daisy. Nice, Daisy. *(Relaxes a bit.)* Hey, she doesn't seem to mind us.

SAM *(relaxes more)*. This could work.

DARCY. It will work. The Great Samdini and Dee Dee Demento—*(An angry bray from DAISY-HOUDINI. Petrified:)* Uh, Sam? Donkeys don't eat people. Do they?

SAM. Only if they're really, really hungry.

DARCY. Let's hope Daisy ate dinner, then.

(SAM and DARCY look up at Daisy's rump.)

SAM. Deed? Let's hope she didn't.

HOUDINI *(inhaling ambrosia)*. There's nothing quite like the aroma of donkey-doo in the morning. At a truck stop near Tampa, they jumped out of Daisy's trailer, discarded their malodorous clothes, and purchased tasteful resort wear. Then, they caught a bus to Miami, and took a taxi straight to the home of Winston Pawling.

(Sound: a car door slamming, over "Feliz Navidad." HOUDINI dons TAXI DRIVER hat.)

SAM *(offstage)*. Muchas gracias, señor.

TAXI DRIVER-HOUDINI. Feliz Navidad, amigos. (Holds nose.) Ustedes tienen que duchar!

(Dusk. Outside an inviting home, a lovely Christmas tree is seen through the picture window. DARCY and SAM enter in new tacky tourist clothes.)

DARCY. That's his house. *(Resentful.)* Winston Pawling is rich.

SAM. Logical. His parents are doctors. Want to knock?

DARCY. No. Nice Christmas tree. We don't have a Christmas tree.

SAM. It'll be dark soon, Deed, you can't just stand here.

DARCY. Yes I can. It's a free country.

(They sit. A MAN in worn coveralls enters from behind the house. With a squeegee and bucket of water, begins to wash windows.)

DARCY. Look at that. They're SO rich they hire someone to clean their windows. You know who cleans our windows? Me. I bet Winston Pawling is a rich, spoiled brat. *(Dusk fades to night. The Christmas tree glows.)*

HOUDINI. It was Sam's idea to spend the night on the beach. In the morning, they would confront Winston Pawling, rich kid.

(Sound: the ocean.)

DARCY. Can we get arrested for sleeping on the beach?

SAM. Only if we get caught. Did you see those kids sleeping under the pier. Think they're homeless?

DARCY. I guess.

SAM. I kind of miss home. Do you ever think about your parents?

DARCY. No.

SAM. They've been through a lot, Deed. They must be so worried.

DARCY. Since when are you so concerned about my parents? *(Imitating SAM.)* Let's review. Your father is the rich lawyer. My father is the poor cop.

SAM. Where do you get this from? Wait, I know where you—

DARCY. I have my own mind, Sam.

SAM. No you don't. You have your father's mind.

DARCY. At least my father protects innocent people.

SAM. You are so ignorant. My dad is a public defender. Public defenders represent people who are too poor to hire a lawyer.

DARCY. So? Your father doesn't even care if they're guilty or innocent.

SAM. What would your dad do if, right this minute, he saw Mr. Hunter being robbed?

DARCY. Duh. It's his job to protect all people, not just people he likes.

SAM. Duh. My dad, too. That's what a public defender does. And they don't make squat. Why do you think my mom left?

DARCY. I never knew that.

SAM. Well, now you do.

DARCY. I thought lawyers made lots of money.

SAM. Deed, if my father made lots of money, would we live next door to you?

DARCY *(beat)*. Sometimes I hate what comes out of my own mouth.

SAM. Sometimes I hate what comes out of your mouth, too.
(Somewhere someone softly sings "We Three Kings.")

DARCY. Sorry. Adjective. Regret. *(The singing continues as DARCY stares at the night sky.)* What do you think happens to a person, after they die?

SAM. Dunno.

DARCY. Wouldn't it be something if people turned into stars? *(A few other voices join in, "Star of wonder, star of night... ")* I have to tell you something. When you go home tomorrow, I'm not going with you.

SAM. Highly amusing.

DARCY. I can't go home. If you knew what I did.

SAM. What, didn't finish your chores again? *(A beat, as it dawns on him.)* This is about David. About what happened that night. Right? *(The singing stops.)*

HOUDINI *(whispers insistently)*. Tell.

SAM. About what happened when you went to the park.

HOUDINI. Tell.

SAM. You can tell me.

DARCY. I.... I ... can't—

SAM & HOUDINI. You can.

HOUDINI. You must—

DARCY. I can't.

SAM. So you're running away instead? What are you gonna do, go live under the pier?

DARCY. Maybe.

SAM. That's crazy. I'd never see you again.

DARCY. So?

SAM. So? That's all you have to say? So? *(Beat. He looks out at ocean.)* When person A loves person B, person A gets upset at the thought of never seeing person B again.

DARCY *(lying)*. It's better that way. Because person B doesn't love person A back.

(Night turns to morning. Outside the PAWLING home. SAM is hurt and distant. DARCY tries not to care.)

SAM *(coldly)*. Now what?

DARCY. We wait.

SAM. Brilliant.

(The same MAN opens the front door and sweeps.)

DARCY. Look at that. He has to work for them on Christmas Eve.

WINSTON *(calling from inside the house)*. Hey Dad, where are you?

MAN-JOHN PAUL PAWLING *(calling)*. Out here, son!

(DARCY and SAM watch as WINSTON PAWLING comes outside with a football. His dad, DR. JOHN PAUL PAWLING hugs him warmly.)

WINSTON *(fondly)*. You are some kinda clean freak, Dad.

JOHN PAUL *(good-naturedly)*. It's next to godliness, little man.

DARCY. He's twelve?

SAM. That's what the newspaper said.

DARCY. He's even smaller than you, Sam, and you're the smallest twelve-year-old I know.

SAM. Thank you for that observation.

JOHN PAUL *(to WINSTON)*. Remember, you're watching, not playing.

WINSTON. Got it, Dad. See ya.

(JOHN PAUL goes inside. WINSTON tosses football lightly to himself, watches for someone. DARCY is frozen. SAM puts on his oddest sunglasses and crosses to WINSTON, ridiculously ultra-cool.)

SAM. Yo, 'zup?

WINSTON *(thinks SAM is very odd)*. Not much.

SAM. I hear ya, 'brah.

WINSTON. What's up with those sunglasses?

SAM. These? A collector's item. So...want to throw a few?

WINSTON. Nah. I'm going to the beach with my buds for a pick-up game.

SAM. Uh-huh, I'm down with that. *(Beat.)* That's my sister over there. *(Beat.)* We could throw a few while you wait.

WINSTON. Are you any good?

SAM *(indicating DARCY)*. She is. They call her the Fabulous Flying Dee Dee Demento. Chuck her one. *(Calling to DARCY.)* Hey, Demento, think fast!

(WINSTON fires the football to DARCY. She catches it, holds it to her heart. A beat. Slowly, she crosses to him.)

WINSTON *(impressed)*. Decent. *(Wordlessly, DARCY hands him the ball. WINSTON begins a a game of catch with them.)* So, where'd you move here from?

SAM. Europe. Our parents are in the circus.

WINSTON. No way.

SAM. Yuh-way. The Flying Monellas. I'm Sam-Dean Monella. She's Amanda-Bliss Monella.

WINSTON. So why do they call you Dee Dee Demento if your name is Amanda whatever?

SAM. Her full name is Amanda-Bliss-Deirdre Monella, after a bunch of dead relatives. Dee Dee for short. It's a family thing.

WINSTON. Yeah, mine, too. Winston was my grandfather's name. Kids are always asking me if I was named after a pack of cigarettes. I'm like, "both of my parents are doctors. What do you think?"

SAM. Doctors, huh? You want to be a doctor, too?

WINSTON. That's a big N-O. I've spent enough time in hospitals to last me a lifetime.

SAM (*oh-so-innocently*). Oh yeah? How come?

WINSTON. My heart was messed up, so I had to have all this surgery.

DARCY (*very intense*). What kind of surgery?

WINSTON. Just surgery. No biggie. Anyway, I'm fine now.

(*DARCY is hurt, angry. JOHN PAUL steps outside, waters plants, sees WINSTON just as he throws the ball to SAM.*)

JOHN PAUL (*admonishing*). Winston.

WINSTON. That's the first time I threw the ball, Dad, honest.

JOHN PAUL. Just three more months and you can let that ball rip all you want. I thought you were going to the beach to watch Jason and Kenny. (*Beat.*) They didn't come for you, did they?

WINSTON (*hides his hurt*). I guess they got hung up. Whatever.

JOHN PAUL. It'll be different once you're back at school with them. (*Beat.*) Hey, how about we go to early mass?

WINSTON. What about Mom?

JOHN PAUL (*checking his watch*). She called an hour ago and said she was leaving her office.

WINSTON *(teasing).* Yeah, but we're dealing with Planet Mom here.

JOHN PAUL. Tell you what, we'll have lunch and then—

SAM *(hinting).* Lunch! Gee, I'm famished.

WINSTON. This is Sam-Dean and Amanda...something. They just moved here. He says their parents are in the circus.

JOHN PAUL. Welcome to the neighborhood.

SAM *(sniffing).* Do I smell something cooking?

JOHN PAUL *(amused).* Not unless you cooked it. We're having sandwiches and fruit salad. Would you two like to stay for lunch?

SAM. Why, how kind of you to ask.

(Sound: A car stopping, car door slams.)

LINDA PAWLING *(offstage).* Thanks for the lift. Merry Christmas!

JOHN PAUL *(bemused).* Ah, the wife cometh.

(DR. LINDA PAWLING, harried, carries an overflowing briefcase, enters hurriedly from the street.)

LINDA PAWLING *(apologetic).* I know, I know, I'm late. *(Kisses her husband on the cheek.)* But Sarah Scott's grandmother brought her in with strep and then just as I was leaving Mrs. Deering brought Lizzie in with a sprained ankle and then the car wouldn't start and I had to get a lift with—*(She notices DARCY staring at her.)* Hello. Are you a friend of Winston's?

DARCY. No.

JOHN PAUL. This is Amanda. She and her brother Sam-Dean just moved here. Did you call Triple A about your car?

LINDA. All it needs is gas. *(Pulling off her earrings.)* I'll just jump in the shower—I told Mrs. Scott to call if

Sarah's fever spiked, so if she calls tell her I'll call her right back. *(Kisses her husband.)* This is the best Christmas. *(As she enters the house, turns back.)* Oh, nice to meet you, Sam-Dean, and, uh— *(Can't remember DARCY's name.)*

JOHN PAUL. Amanda.

LINDA. Amanda. Merry Christmas, Amanda. *(She goes inside.)*

JOHN PAUL *(to SAM and DARCY)*. Come on in. Wipe your feet. Winston.

(SAM goes inside with him, but DARCY doesn't move.)

DARCY. Why I Hate Winston Pawling, by Darcy Deeton. He's got a Christmas tree. He's rich. He's happy. He's alive.

JOHN PAUL *(sticks his head out, to DARCY, ushering her in)*. Young lady?

(Two hours later. WINSTON and SAM look at WINSTON's videotape collection. A ham radio sits on a table.)

WINSTON. You know this one? *War of the Worlds*? It's classic.

(DARCY enters, anger festering.)

SAM *(too cheerful)*. Hey, sis. That was some lunch, huh?

WINSTON. I guess she didn't think so. She didn't eat anything.

DARCY *(cold)*. I lost my appetite.

WINSTON. Want to check out my ham radio? I built it. It's called a transceiver.

DARCY *(disdain)*. Like what truck drivers use or something?

WINSTON *(turns the ham radio on, fiddles with the dial).* That's citizens band radio. For ham radio, you have to pass a test and get a license. And you can talk to people all over the world. Maybe even other worlds.

(He turns up the radio. Sound: a babble of voices. JOHN PAUL enters, impeccably dressed in suit and tie. He carries water and pills, which he hands to WINSTON, who takes the pills surreptitiously. JOHN PAUL turns off the radio.)

JOHN PAUL. Winston's pretty convinced there's life out there.

WINSTON. There is, Dad. I just read this great book about this alien who comes to Earth, by this guy Robert Heinlein, called—

DARCY. *Stranger in a Strange Land.* Book number twenty-three.

SAM. Sis numbers her books. She's kinda quirky. But we love her.

(Carolers outside sing. LINDA hurries in, dressed in something colorful and flowing, without shoes.)

LINDA. Carolers! They're right outside! *(She goes to the window, opens it, sings along lightly.)*

WINSTON. You forgot your shoes, Mom.

LINDA. I just can't find the ones that go with—*(Carolers change songs, continue singing under scene.)* I love this one. We should go out and sing with them.

JOHN PAUL. We're leaving for mass in a half hour, sharp. Maybe we can actually get to this one. *(Caroling fades.)*

LINDA *(referring to the carolers)*. They're leaving. *(Calling.)* Thanks, that was so great! Merry Christmas!

CAROLERS *(offstage)*. Merry Christmas!

JOHN PAUL. Winston, I'm sure your guests have to get home for—

LINDA. Listen, has anyone seen my purple sandals?

WINSTON. Under the couch in the family room.

LINDA. Thanks, sweetie. *(She exits.)*

JOHN PAUL. You children will need to excuse us so that Winston can get changed for—

DARCY *(bitter)*. Church. You're going to church. So you can pray.

JOHN PAUL. Yes.

DARCY *(still bitter)*. So you can thank God for your blessings. But you never think about who suffered for your blessings, do you?

JOHN PAUL. Oh, but I do. I thank Jesus every time I look at my son. Now, do you kids need a ride home?

SAM. No, thanks. Before we go, I think Amanda-Bliss-Deirdre has something she wants to tell you.

DARCY. No.

SAM. Yes.

DARCY. Just leave me alone.

SAM. Here's how you start: My name's not really Amanda.

JOHN PAUL. I don't understand. Winston?

WINSTON *(bewildered)*. Got me.

(LINDA enters.)

SAM. —Tell them, Deed.

LINDA. Tell us what?

DARCY. No.

SAM. You have to.

LINDA. Winston?

(WINSTON shrugs, perplexed.)

DARCY. I said no.

SAM. Tell them—

HOUDINI. Tell them—

DARCY. No.

SAM. You can do it—

HOUDINI. You can do it—

DARCY *(backing away)*. Leave me alone.

SAM. My name is...

DARCY. No!

SAM & HOUDINI. My name is...

DARCY *(torn from her)*. NO!

SAM & HOUDINI *(relentless, until DARCY cracks)*. My name is... my name is... my name is—

DARCY. My name is Darcy Deeton! My brother was David Deeton. And you don't even know who that is!

(But she's wrong, they do know.)

JOHN PAUL. Oh, Lord.

LINDA. Darcy, we—

DARCY. You live here in your perfect house with your perfect lives and you don't even know what you have. Do you know what my family has? Nothing. *(Turns on WINSTON.)* But you! You have everything. Even my brother's heart. And you don't even know his name.

(JOHN PAUL takes a step toward DARCY and holds out his arms. LINDA holds WINSTON.)

JOHN PAUL. Darcy...

DARCY *(savagely)*. Stay away from me!

JOHN PAUL. I understand. I know how much you're hurting.

DARCY. You don't know anything. I deserve to hurt. I deserve to die.

LINDA. No—

DARCY. I do. Because I killed him. *(Beats of silence, as that night comes back to DARCY. Then, she relives it all.)* It was my birthday. I got mad at him. I said: "I wish you were dead!" and I ran away. He ran after me, between the parked cars...then I heard these terrible sounds...a car. A thud. A crash. I couldn't turn around. Oh God, I couldn't turn around!

JOHN PAUL *(takes DARCY in his arms, crying with her, rocking her).* Shhhhhh. It's okay. It's okay, now.

DARCY. I didn't mean to. Please God, I didn't mean to.

JOHN PAUL. God knows. I believe that with all my heart. You can lay your burden down now. God knows. And He forgives.

DARCY. You don't understand. It's not God I need to forgive me. It's David. *(This agony touches LINDA so deeply that she leaves her son, crosses to DARCY, and puts her arms around both DARCY and her husband. DARCY continues, weeping.)* It's David...

(As the PAWLINGS rock DARCY, HOUDINI looks on. Fade to black. Night. The backyard. The upstage platform now serves as the tree house. WINSTON and SAM sit downstage. DARCY enters self-consciously.)

DARCY. Hi. *(Beat.)* I fell asleep, I guess. Where're your parents?

WINSTON. In the bedroom.

DARCY. They wanted to go to church.

WINSTON. S'okay. Dad said to get you something to eat when you woke up. Be right back. *(He exits.)*

SAM. So. I called my dad. He hyperventilated. But he said he'd meet our plane tomorrow in Green Bay.

DARCY. What plane?

SAM. The one Winston's parents are paying for. They insisted. *(Beat.)* We called your parents, too.

DARCY. Your dad would have called them, anyway.

SAM. Deed. I told your dad what happened that night. I know I didn't have the right to. But you'd run away forever before you'd tell him. I couldn't let you do it. I'd rather let you hate me.

DARCY *(a beat)*. What did he say?

SAM. Not much.

(WINSTON enters with fruit, hands some to DARCY and SAM.)

WINSTON. You wanna eat up in my tree house? My parents built it. See, how they built around the palm tree so they wouldn't hurt it?

SAM. Ingenious. Adjective. Clever invention.

(WINSTON climbs up easily, and SAM follows, and then DARCY does too, but reluctantly. She tries to ignore the following conversation.)

WINSTON *(showing SAM a photo)*. This is my T-ball baseball team from when I was seven. That's me, right there.

SAM *(re the photo)*. What kind of team name is "The House of Pain"?

WINSTON. Paine's Furniture Store was our team sponsor. We took first in our division. In the last game, bottom of the sixth, Earl's Hardware is up on us, 8-6. With guys on first and second, I hit this line drive in the gap. The left fielder finally gets it, fires to the cut-off man, he lets it get through his legs, one guy scores, then another. First baseman finally throws home. I slide under the tag. It was awesome. *(He pulls down a tarp that covers some framed photos on a tree house wall.)*

SAM. Excellent. A photo gallery.

WINSTON. Of my all-time heroes. That's Neil Armstrong, the first astronaut to walk on the moon. That's Carl Sagan, he was this amazing astronomer. That's Jackie Robinson—I guess you know who he is. *(Beat.)* And that's ... David Deeton.

(This gets DARCY's attention. Her eyes lock on the photo.)

DARCY. David.

WINSTON. After my parents found out whose heart I got, they tracked down a newspaper article about David with that photo. Mom put it next to my hospital bed. When I came home, it came home, too.

DARCY. You could have written to my parents. Something.

WINSTON. Yeah, but ... *(Beat.)* When I was seven, the doctor said I couldn't play sports anymore. Then after a while, I couldn't do anything anymore. That's when my dad started carrying me up here. I'd stare up at the stars making deals with God. Like, "God, if you give me just one year to be like everyone else, I'll give you anything you want."

SAM. An equitable proffer.

WINSTON. I guess God didn't think so. I just got sicker.

DARCY. And then you got David's heart?

WINSTON *(nods)*. When I woke up and I felt his heart beating inside of me, for the first time since I was six years old, I felt young again. And strong.

DARCY. You could have written that to my parents.

WINSTON. No one wants to get a letter from someone they hate.

SAM. Why would they hate you?

WINSTON. Because I'm so happy to be alive. But I'm only alive because their son is...*(Impassioned, to DARCY.)* I think about your brother all the time. All the time.
(Silence. DARCY lays down, stares out at the night sky. She points to something.)

DARCY. See that red star up there? That's—

DARCY, SAM & WINSTON. Betelgeuse. *(They look at each other with wonder. WINSTON and SAM lay down too, looking at the sky.)*

WINSTON. It's five-hundred and twenty-seven light years from Earth.

DARCY. Even if it died tonight, its light would keep on shining for the next five-hundred and twenty-seven years. *(Beat.)* Winston? Could I listen to my brother's heart?
(Slowly, WINSTON nods. DARCY gently puts her head on WINSTON's chest.)

SAM. Can you hear it, Deed?

DARCY *(smiling through tears)*. It's so wonderful, Sam. *(To DAVID's heart.)* I love you, David. And I miss you so much. I'll remember what you taught me for the next five hundred and twenty-seven years. I'll teach it to my children, and they'll teach it to their children, so your light will never go out. Thank you for being the greatest brother in the world. And most of all, thank you for saving Winston's life. *(DARCY sits up. Her face changes— radiant wonder.)* Sam! Oh, Sam, I hear David!

SAM *(puts hand on WINSTON's heart)*. Here?

DARCY *(puts hand on own heart)*. No. Here.

WINSTON. What's he saying?

DARCY. He's saying: "Darce, I forgive you." *(To WIN-STON.)* I forgive you.

(Beats of silence, and then a heartbeat segues into a whisper of ham radio voices which grows louder, a babble of loving voices in every tongue.)

HOUDINI. Dear audience, it's almost midnight now. The truth is, days passed, years vanished, and I walked, blind and deaf to a miracle. It took a little girl in a tree house to teach me: when I listen with my heart, my mother is always with me.

(As HOUDINI speaks, DARCY, back home now, crosses into Meemaw's room. HOUDINI and DARCY's lines practically overlap.)

DARCY. Merry Christmas, Meemaw. Betelgeuse is out tonight.

HOUDINI. How I shall miss your faces! Look for me...

DARCY. I showed Dad.

HOUDINI *(points to the stars)*. —there.

DARCY. You should have told him that you were proud of him.

HOUDINI. And listen for me—

DARCY. It would have meant so much to him.

HOUDINI & DARCY *(hands on their heart, simultaneously)*. —here.

(HOUDINI makes a magic butterfly appear, and as it flies away and disappears, so does he. DARCY pulls a chair up to Meemaw's bed.)

DARCY. I wanted to see you while it's still Christmas. You must wonder why David stopped coming to see you. He was in an accident. I'm sorry to have to tell you, but David is dead. In one way, though, he'll never die. *(She opens a worn paperback.)* I'm reading book twenty-eight on your list, *The Member of the Wedding.* I thought I'd start at my favorite part and read a little to you each time I see you, and then we can read the end together. *(A clock strikes midnight, the lights slowly begin to fade. Reading:)* "Frankie stood looking into the sky. For when the old question came to her—the who she was and what she would be in the world, and why she was standing there that minute—when the old question came to her, she did not feel hurt and unanswered. At last she knew just who she was and understood where she was going. She loved her brother and the bride and she was a member of the wedding. The three of them would go into the world and they would always be together. And finally, after the scared spring and the crazy summer, she was no more afraid."

(Now, the only light is the bright red glow of Betelgeuse shining above. Then, in a split second, the ceiling of the theatre is illuminated by thousands of magical twinkling white stars, surrounding the red light of Betelgeuse.)

THE END

DIRECTOR'S NOTES

DIRECTOR'S NOTES

DIRECTOR'S NOTES

DIRECTOR'S NOTES

DIRECTOR'S NOTES